Sorrow's Joy

THE TRUE STORY OF A BROTHER AND SISTER AT GETTYSBURG

By Meara Kelly
Illustrated by Jeanette Dillard

***

This story is lovingly dedicated to my family. Because of them, my sorrows are not lonely and my joys are so much sweeter.

***

CONTENTS

	Acknowledgements	VII
	Illustrator's Note	IX
1	My Town	1
2	Do What's Right	11
3	Pieces of News	25
4	A Mission for Me	39
5	Friday, June 26, 1863	48
6	Three Days of Thunder	65
7	Yea, Though I Walk	82
8	Finding Joy	90

ACKNOWLEDGMENTS

Cindy L. Small author of "The Jennie Wade Story" where I gained much of my information about Jennie and Gettysburg for this story.
Kristen Stieffel who went above and beyond in editing this story to get it ready to be published.
My extremely talented illustrator, Jeanette Dillard, who made this story come to life before my very eyes.

Illustrator's Note About The Flower on the Cover

The symbol of hope is light: piercing, shattering, and ultimately inspiring. Sometimes, it is so bright that it fills earth's space completely; at other times, hope shines alone in defiance to darkness. The Nasturtium is a red, spindly flower that grows freely in most soils around the world, originating in South America and imported to Europe around the 16th century. Resembling the trophy pole that ancient Roman victors hung the battered shields and blood-stained helmets of their foes, the Nasturtium traditionally represents courage and victory in battle or conquest. Although tragic, the story of Jennie Wade resounds with undefeated strength and undying bravery in a time of doubt, departure, and death. It sounds strange to admit that the darkest stories teach us to hope, but history rings with the tales of individuals who inspired the world when kindness alone gave them the courage to shine.

My Town

WHEN SOMEONE THINKS OF GETTYSBURG, they tend to imagine the battle that raged there from July first to the third in the year 1863. My mind also wanders to those days because I lived through them. My family and I hid in a house, our ears ringing from the constant noise of cannons and gun shots. The worst three days of my life.

But there was so much more to Gettysburg than a battle. Before it was linked to the War Between the States, it was a town just like every other town. It was a quaint place, surrounded by beautiful mountains that seemed to shelter it from harm. Shops and houses lined the streets. People would pass and greet one another on sunny mornings as the town became alive with bustling shoppers. Many proud farmers would claim that their bumper crop was more prosperous than those of their neighbors. But this was always in fun. Even though farming was a large part of Gettysburg's economy, the carriage-making industry and a spinning wheel factory flourished, which also gave the town something to boast about.

Sorrow's Joy

Long before the thought of a war was considered, much less a battle in our backyards, something exciting came to town. As a rambunctious boy, I ran down the street toward the Diamond, our town square. It had been named by the founder of Gettysburg, James Gettys, way back in 1786, when he sketched out the town and included a square in the center of it with a plan for buildings to spring up around it. And that is exactly what happened.

I had almost reached the Diamond when I noticed a crowd of people gathered in the middle of the street. As I got closer, I saw they were discussing something. I laughed, because no one was listening to anyone else. How in the world did they know what they were discussing? But when I drew nearer, I could quickly tell that they were all taking about the same thing: the railroad coming to Gettysburg.

Mrs. Tanner, a woman in her late sixties who had mentioned many times in the past that she feared uncertainties, said, "It will surely change our town."

"Change in a good way," a man chimed in.

"Just think," Elizabeth Crawford mused half to herself and partly so everyone could hear her, "new people and shipments coming right through our own town. How exciting!"

The voices continued to rise and fall as people grew more passionate or fearful, whispering to their neighbor thoughts on the subject they did not want others to hear. I squeezed in between Mr. and Mrs.

My Town

Welty in hopes of hearing more of the conversation. The thought of a railroad and change excited me. I looked across at the people in front of me and caught a glimpse of my friend Franklin standing in the middle of that crowd. He noticed me too and motioned me over.

"A lot of people are talking about the railroad," he said in a loud voice to be heard above the crowd.

"Yes," I said. "Is the railroad coming next week?"

Franklin rolled his eyes. He enjoyed exploiting the fact that he knew more than me because he was fortunate enough to have been born five years before me. "Samuel," he said slowly, "it takes years to build a railroad. They're going to start building next week, but it'll be a long time before they're done."

"Oh."

"It won't be the only railroad that goes through our town," Franklin had lowered his voice so I could barely hear him, but by his mannerisms I knew this was something I did not want to miss.

I leaned in closer. "What do you mean?"

Even though both Franklin and I knew no adults would want to listen in on two young boys' conversation, he looked around to make sure no one was overhearing him, just for effect.

"Don't tell me you don't know that we have an underground railroad in our town," he said, in a haughty way.

My eyes lowered and I peered down at my feet. "There's a railroad below us?" I wondered why I had never heard the rumble or felt the earth shake beneath me as the train roared through.

This time Franklin let out a laugh. "No, no, not an actual railroad!" He laughed some more at my bewilderment. "The Underground Railroad isn't a railroad at all. It's a path runaway slaves take to escape to freedom."

Now I understood why Franklin had lowered his voice. Gettysburg was certainly divided on the issue of slavery. Since we were so close to slave territory, some people supported the institution.

Franklin continued. "But I've secretly heard that since we are so close to the slave states, our town is a vital stop for the Underground Railroad. No one is really supposed to know this or which houses are stops, but I know for a fact that what I'm saying is true. I saw runaway slaves once."

"When? Where?" I asked.

Grateful that he had my full attention, Franklin continued in dramatic tones. "Well, I was out one night walking home from Jeremy's house. I must admit it was pretty late. I passed by the Welty's house and I saw two figures at their door. It was dark, so I couldn't make out who they were. The Welty's house is so far from the main road, so I crept closer. Since I didn't want them to see me, I hid behind their big old tree. I nearly let out a yelp when I saw they were African, and I understood why they were at the Welty's door."

"What did they look like?" I asked in awe that Franklin had seen actual runaway slaves.

"They looked as if they would collapse at any minute, and their clothes were torn and muddy. The man even had to steady the woman. I suspect they were married—running away because they were going to be separated. I also suspect that the slave catcher and his dogs had been chasing them for heaven knows how long."

"Then what happened?" I asked. "Were they let inside right away to hide?"

"I wish I could say they were." Franklin shook his head. "But that was not the case. They stayed by the door, looking more and more nervous as it remained shut. I saw the man look up into the sky and ask the woman in a frantic tone, 'What's we gonna do?' The woman took one look at him and whispered, 'Knock again.' The man did. Three short knocks. Tap, tap, tap. It seemed like ages before I noticed a small light in the window. They saw it too. Then the door quickly opened and Mr. Welty ushered them in."

"Then what?" I asked, completely engulfed in the story and completely forgetting that we were surrounded by a group of chattering townsfolk.

Sorrow's Joy

They looked as if they would collapse at any minute

My Town

"Then what? What else is there to tell? They went inside and there was no way I was going to peek through the window and be accused of being a slave catcher! I went home."

I looked across at Mr. and Mrs. Welty as they talked and laughed with their neighbors. Who knew they had such a secret! How many other slaves had they helped escape to freedom under the cover of darkness while the rest of the town slept soundly in their beds? Everyone that is, except Franklin.

"Yeah, so I don't think this normal railroad is anything to get excited about," Franklin explained. "A lot of towns have railroads, but our town is one of the few to have an Underground Railroad."

I agreed. I never looked at the Welty's tiny yellow house the same way again. How many secrets did it hold?

However, when the railroad did spring up a year later, for a time I forgot all about this Underground Railroad and replaced it with expectation of the sound of a whistle way off in the distance. What surprises would this train hold? Would it have a new shipment for the general store, or a long awaited guest? Would Gettysburg just be a stopping point so the train could travel to bigger better cities such as, Harrisburg, Philadelphia, and Baltimore? Gettysburg had something else to be proud about: we were now linked to these major cities.

***

Many who lived in Gettysburg would say that the railroad making an appearance in their fair town was the most monumental event. However, I know a girl who would disagree with them.

Before a railroad above or below the ground was even thought about, Jennie waited outside her home on a hot August day. She waited for a sound. She hardly noticed her friend, Jack, walking up the path. He whistled a familiar tune everyone in town linked to him since it came from his lips so often. He held a pail and a fishing pole as his lanky legs carried him. His hair was all in shambles and he was hatless, not a surprise to most who knew he always lost his cap while fishing.

He sat down next to her. Jack knew her mind was on something terribly important because she didn't even greet him. "Hasn't happened yet?"

"Not yet." Her eyes fixed straight ahead.

"It's kind of hot out here." Jack shaded his eyes from the sun. "What I'd do for a glass of lemonade."

The girl finally looked at him. "Well, I wish I could offer to get you some, but I'm not allowed in the house."

"She is older than you." Jack picked up a piece of wood and started whittling.

"Only by a year! Why does Georgia get to help in there and not me?"

"I don't know. When you get adults figured out and all their rules and regulations, you let me know," Jack said with a smile.

The girl smiled back and took the piece of wood from his hands and ran her hand along the edges.

"Where's John?" Jack asked, referring to her younger brother.

"Oh, he's out in the back playing," she answered.

"In any event"—Jack stood up—"it's an exciting day for you."

She nodded with the same intense look on her face she had when he arrived.

"So," Jack said in a teasing tone, "be happy! What's that pensive look for?"

"I'm waiting," she replied with defiance. "I can't relax until I hear that sound."

Almost as if she had ordered it herself, the sound came through the closed window. A muffled cry. She jumped to her feet.

"There it is! There it is!" She grabbed Jack, startling him, and whirled him around. "And here I am. The big sister!"

Moments later, a tiny red-faced baby boy was placed in her arms. She folded back the blanket and peered at his peaceful sleeping face.

Sorrow's Joy

"We're going to call him Samuel," Mama said from over the bed.

"A perfect name," she cooed, "for my little brother."

So this day happened to be a very important one to me as well. Not just because it was the day I was born, but because it was the day Jennie became my sister.

Do What's Right

WHY DID I EVER TAKE A JOB as delivery boy for James Pierce's butcher shop? I hated the strong, irresistible smell of the shop. Mr. Pierce was an unfriendly man with an incurable scowl on his face. But he wouldn't fire me, because no other boy in the town of Gettysburg would be crazy enough to work for sour old Mr. Pierce.

I was twelve years old then, and in addition to my age, much had changed. Yes, the railroad still roared through our town, and I felt the same excitement of something new that was coming whenever I heard it way off in the distance. I assumed the Underground Railroad was still a secret part of our town. Mr. and Mrs. Welty were much older now, but they were as vivacious as ever. The issue of slavery still made people uncomfortable, angry, sad, or defiant. Slavery and the question of states' rights were linked to a war that seemed to have started a hundred thousand miles away in Charleston, South Carolina, three years ago.

I left for work in a timely manner that morning. My

house and the butcher shop were both on Breckenridge Street. Most of the time, I had to rush to work, but not that morning. As I walked along the dirt streets I smiled to myself, since I could enjoy the scenery instead of it rushing pass me. Spring was leaving us, as this June morning was rather warm. Yes, today would be a good day.

Before my feet were in the door, Mr. Pierce started barking orders.

There went my good day.

"You are here, Samuel," he rumbled as if I had been late. "There is much to do today."

"Yes, sir," I grabbed my white apron from its peg.

"No, no." Mr. Pierce shook his head. "We have some early morning deliveries to make today. First, you must go to John Winebrenner's shop and then, since it's on the same street, I need you to deliver a pound a beef to Mrs. Welty. Finish at Mrs. McCreary, and come back after that and pick up more deliveries."

I nodded, grabbed the meat on the counter and ran out the door.

My first delivery was for John Winebrenner, a friendly tanner. I walked in the door and Mr. Winebrenner looked up and smiled as the bell above the door gave a little jingle. "Samuel! It's so good to see you."

I noticed he was in the beginning process of making leather as he softened a hide by hitting it with a mace—a four-sided piece of wood on a long pole. It was used specifically for making leather smooth.

Each time I walked into his shop, disappointment hit me. I wanted to work for him, but before I was able to ask, Franklin had snatched the job and was now happily employed by this pleasant and patient man. Mr. Winebrenner had to be patient; the process of making leather could take two years! The shop had the awful smell of decaying animals, but the tanner's job was very important, especially for farmers to make their saddles and bridles, and Mr. Winebrenner was pleased to help the townsfolk.

As I stepped into the shop, Franklin came out of the back room. I took one step back. My wonder at this older and smarter boy, who always liked to point out these qualities, had left me long ago. Now I just found him annoying.

"Oh, hello, Samuel," he said, in what I took as a condescending way.

"Hello," I answered coldly, and then turned to Mr. Winebrenner. "I have your delivery, sir."

"Oh, thanks, thanks." Mr. Winebrenner continued with his work. "The wife will be happy it got here early. The tip's on the counter, Samuel."

I thanked him, picked up the tip, and left. I was soon walking along Baltimore Street on my way to the Welty household. I stopped in front of their house and wondered how many runaway slaves had stood right where I was standing as they trembled in the night.

Mrs. Welty opened the door. "Come in, Samuel."

I wiped my feet. "Hello, Mrs. Welty." I looked around their small house. Where on earth did they hide the slaves? Maybe they had hidden rooms behind their tall bookshelves.

"I said, do you have the meat, Samuel?" Mrs. Welty asked.

"I wasn't paying attention," I apologized. "Sorry." I handed her the meat.

"Thank you," she said. "I'm making a special vegetable stew tonight." She smiled and stepped into her kitchen. I followed her.

"Are you having company tonight, ma'am?" It really was not an errand boy's business to question, but she didn't seem to care.

"No, no," she answered. "Today is Solomon's birthday, and this stew is his favorite."

I left her house, just as I always did, without a single clue of their home being a stop for the Underground Railroad.

All my deliveries were going well, and I considered the thought that this was going to turn out to be a good day after all, even with Mr. Pierce's grouchiness and the bother of seeing Franklin at the place I wanted to work. Maybe I would even get my deliveries and the rest of my work finished quickly and go home early. However, my third delivery, to Mrs. McCreary, took much longer than expected. She was a very nervous woman and had heard rumors that there would soon be a battle between the blue and gray in our little town. Of course, when I stopped at her home to deliver her order, I asked how she was.

She flew into a panic. "In a few days time, Gettysburg will be no more!" She wailed. "The people of our fair town will be scattered about or worse...dead!" She informed me that just the day before, June 15, Governor Andrew G. Curtin had sent a telegram suggesting that citizens move their stores to safer locations as soon as possible.

"Isn't that just like a politician?" Mrs. McCreary grumbled. "Being so disconnected with the people! How does he expect the businessmen and farmers of Gettysburg to move their supplies in so short a time? And is any place really, truly safe?"

I couldn't blame her for her fears. The War Between the States occupied most of our time, thoughts, and prayers. Rumors of a battle happening right outside our doors had been going around for months.

Mrs. McCreary's two sons just survived the Battle of Chancellorsville back in April. Unfortunately, they were fighting on opposite sides. Everyone felt sorry for this poor woman who had to say good-bye to both her sons, David and Matthew, as they left wearing different uniforms. Mrs. McCreary was heartbroken, not just because she feared for her sons, but because they were fighting against one another.

"When my boys were young," Mrs. McCreary would tell her neighbors, "and they got into an argument, I was always there to help them work it out. They would do so and go back to being friends. Now there is nothing I can do to fix this disagreement, and if they both live to the end of this war, I doubt if they will ever be friends again."

My family was also caught up in the war effort. My oldest sister's husband, John Louis McClellan, was serving with the 165th Pennsylvania Volunteers regiment. In addition, my other sister's fiancé, Jack Skelly, whom she had been friends with for years, was fighting with the Eighth Corps in Virginia.

I sat down with Mrs. McCreary to try to calm her. She was grateful and offered me some lemonade, and I politely accepted. We talked on her front porch awhile, and before I knew it, time had slipped past. I jumped up from the porch, said a hurried good-bye to Mrs. McCreary, and raced down the street.

"This is not going to turn out well. This is not going to turn out well," I said over and over to myself as my feet took me as fast as they could back to the butcher's shop. Thankfully, Mr. Pierce had given me a note with the rest of the deliveries I had to make. All I had to do was to sneak into the shop, undetected by Mr. Pierce, get the meat, and finish the deliveries. Maybe he had forgotten all about me and that I had not come back yet because he was busy with work.

Do What's Right

Much to my disadvantage though, Mr. Pierce was an astute man who always knew the time and what was going on around him, even when it looked as if his job would take up all of his thoughts. Because of this, I decided to slip in the back door and quietly steal into the room where the meat was kept. I only hoped that Mr. Pierce was with a customer when I got there. Thankfully, he was. The only problem was that I had to walk silently behind him to get to the meat.

Mr. Pierce was helping Catherine Snyder decide what kind of meat she wanted. I breathed a sigh of relief, knowing that he was very busy at this point and he would probably not hear me. Miss Snyder was our most particular customer. She never came knowing what she wanted, and when she did decide, she always had at least a hundred questions to ask about the cut of the meat, how fresh it was, how much she would need for the dish she was making. As Miss Snyder kept showering questions on poor Mr. Pierce, who just wanted to package up her meat and send her on her way, I tip-toed behind him, careful not to let the floor squeak as I eyed my destination.

Miss Snyder looked up and her eyes fell on me.

"Oh, hello Sam—" She stopped midsentence as I made motions demonstrating I did not want Mr. Pierce to know I was there.

"What was that, Miss Snyder?" Mr. Pierce wearily asked, as if he had not been listening to her for the past five minutes.

"Oh, nothing, Mr. Pierce." She replied. "I was just wondering if you have any salmon?"

"No, ma'am, we do not."

"Then I'll be on my way," Miss Snyder smiled and walked out the door.

By then, I had raced out the back. I don't think Mr. Pierce saw me.

I made the rest of my deliveries to some very angry customers. When I was conscious enough to recognize what time it was, I realized that Mr. Pierce's shop had already closed. Unfortunately, since my house was on the same street, I had to pass the butcher shop to return home. It was dark, thankfully. As I walked by the shop on the other side of the street, I did see that inside, by the light of a faint gas lamp, Mr. Pierce was sweeping the shop, which was usually my job. A guilty pain swept through my body. I should walk across the street, step into the shop, and take the broom from Mr. Pierce's hand, but he would be extremely angry at me and maybe even fire me.

I knew exactly what he would say: *Samuel, you are an irresponsible young man, and I am extremely disappointed in you.*

So, with a heavy heart, slow steps, and a downcast head, I made the rest of my journey home. Any other day I was always happy to return from a long day at work to my cheerful home. My youngest brother,

Harry, who was eight, would run up, greet me, and then go into a long explanation of what his day entailed. However, this day I was in no mood to listen to him, so I walked past Harry, who wrinkled his forehead.

"What is wrong with you?" My oldest brother, John, asked when I entered the living room. He was sitting on the sofa reading and looked up just in time to catch the sorry look on my face.

"Nothing," I snapped. "Where's Jennie?"

As John turned back to his book, he pointed to the kitchen. I should have guessed. If Jennie wasn't in the garden, she was usually in the kitchen. As I walked into the room I saw her by the stove stirring some soup. She looked up and smiled as she heard my footsteps. Her smile could light up a whole room. Jennie had the kind of personality that made others want to be near her. She had to take over most of the household duties ever since my oldest sister, Georgia, left a year ago, after she got married. She was now expecting a child, and my mother spent a good amount of time at her house over on Baltimore Street.

Jennie had a lot on her mind ever since the war began and Jack Skelly left. Even though Jennie was chipper and helpful as ever, I knew she worried about him. Once in a while I would see her sitting at the windowsill looking out into the long street, and I knew she must be hoping she might catch a glimpse of Jack walking to our house, as he had done so many

Sorrow's Joy

She looked up and smiled

times.

"What's bothering you, Samuel?" Jennie asked, interrupting my thoughts.

I wanted to answer *nothing* and quietly busy myself in the kitchen. Nevertheless, feeling as though I might burst into tears at any moment, I poured out the whole story of my desire to be on time, the delay at Mrs. McCreary's, my rush to finish the deliveries, and my choice not to set foot in the shop after my tardiness.

Jennie listened to my story without a word.

After I had finished, I pulled up a chair, plopped down and cupped my hands over my face. You would think, by the way I responded to this whole ordeal, that I was a baby, a softy, a chicken, and overacting, but I took my job very seriously and hated when people were disappointed in me.

"You know, Sam..." Jennie pulled up a chair next to me and laid a hand on my shoulder. "You are going to have to go to work tomorrow and explain to Mr. Pierce."

"I can't," I shot back. "Mr. Pierce will be so angry with me...I'm afraid to face him and explain."

"But Sam, you know deep down inside you have to go to work. You cannot spend the rest of your life avoiding what needs to be done. Sometimes doing right is the most terrifying thing, but that doesn't mean you should escape from it."

Sorrow's Joy

I kept my eyes downcast, not wanting to look up into Jennie's face.

"Sam," she continued, "you need to do what's right, even if it scares you."

At that moment, I knew all that Jennie was saying was true, and I needed to face Mr. Pierce. I nodded and produced a slight smile to let Jennie know I understood what she was telling me. Jennie smiled back and gave my hand a squeeze.

"Now." She stood. "Let's eat some dinner, shall we?"

***

I took a deep breath before entering the shop the next morning. Mr. Pierce did not look up when he heard the tiny bell jingle as I stepped in. I walked to the back of the store and took my white apron off its hanger. Why hadn't Mr. Pierce followed me and demanded an explanation for yesterday? As I went to the front of the store, Mr. Pierce grunted a greeting as he always did. I couldn't take it any longer. I wanted my confessing to be over with so I could go on with the rest of the day.

"Mr. Pierce?" I stepped closer to him.

He looked up.

"Even if you're not going to mention it, I would like to explain about yesterday and tell you why I didn't return from my deliveries last night." I told him all I had told Jennie, making sure not to leave anything out.

After I was done, Mr. Pierce nodded slowly. "When you didn't come back last night, I assumed you had taken the money from the deliveries and had no intention of bringing it to me. I was prepared to come to your home and have a little talk with your mother and then dismiss you. However, just before I made my way to your house, Mrs. McCreary stopped me in the street and had nothing but good things to say about you. She was very grateful that you took the time to calm her nerves. She said you were just what she needed at that time, and that you were all she would want in a delivery boy."

I was beaming, and we could have left it at that, but I still thought the rest of the story should be explained. "Sir, it is true that I felt sorry for Mrs. McCreary and wanted to help her. Because of that, I was late for the rest of my deliveries, which I am sorry for. I have to admit, I was scared of what you might think, so…even though I could have, I didn't come back to the shop."

"I thought as much when I talked to Mrs. McCreary," Mr. Pierce answered. "Next time, in any situation, for any reason, come to me." With that, Mr. Pierce went back to his work. I stood there for a moment or two with a smile on my face, looking at Mr. Pierce in a new light.

Later that morning, when he sent me out to make some deliveries, he stopped me at the door. "Samuel, you are very involved in the war, correct?"

"Yes, sir," I answered. "My brother-in-law is fighting and so is a family friend. I only wish I could fight myself or do something for the cause."

"All right." Mr. Pierce turned around. "On your way now."

Pieces of News

SATURDAY MORNING, JUNE 20, 1863, was bright and extremely sunny. Jennie and Harry and I walked down the street, heading home from a long day of shopping. I held the basket as Jennie held firmly onto Harry's hand. If she did not do this, Harry would run off and it would take hours to find him. That happened a lot. As we walked, I saw many faces I recognized, and Jennie greeted our friends.

I saw one person I knew sitting on the side of the street as if he was watching the world pass him. Jeremiah was his name. He was just my age, but we were not really friends. I attributed this to the fact that his life and mine were so different. Yes, we both lived in Gettysburg, but he had come here with his family three years ago from Virginia. He used to live on a plantation, but not in the fancy white house with a wrap-around porch you sometimes see in photographs. He lived on the other side of the plantation in a wooden shack and would roll off his mat before dawn to pick cotton day after day. You see, he used to be slave. That was until he, his father, his mother, and his little sister made a daring escape. Once, Jeremiah told me about their flight.

"It was scary," he confessed. "We used to rest during the day and run at night. When we were still close to the plantation, our master sent out his dogs to find us. At that point we all scurried up a tree. My papa had just boosted me up when the sound of the dogs came closer and closer. He climbed to the top just in time. I never been so afraid in my life! Them dogs sniffed all around the tree. We could all barely breathe, and we didn't wanna just in case they heard us. Thank the good Lord them dogs was kind of dumb, 'cause they never found us."

Jeremiah would also tell me about life on the plantation.

"It was hard work. Hot, hard work. We never saw our master much. There was rumors he wasn't such a bad man, but we all doubted that, 'cause why would a nice man hire such a horrible overseer? He was an evil man who seemed to just watch us to make sure no mistakes was made. And, of course, no one is perfect. Mistakes was made, and I saw too many people beaten."

Jeremiah shook his head and stared off into the distance as if he could see, all the way from Gettysburg, the plantation in Virginia with its rows and rows of snow white cotton and his people bent over as the sun beat down on their backs, picking and picking in order to make another man rich.

Pieces of News

"Jeremiah?" I asked.

He turned, and I found myself looking into his piercing dark eyes. "Did you ever have any good times in Virginia? Was it all bad?"

He sighed and smiled a little. "Some," he admitted. "You see, my mama and I had a little game we would play. Soon as I was old enough to work in the fields I learned I would die from discouragement 'fore too long. As the days wore on, I could hardly get off my mat when the sun would peep over the horizon. I could not face another day."

"What did you do?" I could only understand Jeremiah's troubles in light of me not wanting to get out of bed in the morning because of chores I had to do that day, but these could not compare to his labor.

"Mama knew how much I was strugglin'," Jeremiah answered. "So, she came up with a game we played each and every day to get through that day."

"What was it?"

He smiled. "Seems like kid stuff, but it helped. Every day we would try to find at least one thing to be joyful about. From big things like a weddin' or gettin' our work done early to small things like the sun not shinin' so hot or rest on the Sabbath. On days we couldn't think of anythin' we rejoiced that the good Lord was comin' soon."

"I can't imagine finding joy if you're a slave," I remarked.

"It ain't easy." Jeremiah shook his head. "But that's the joy worth tellin'; the joy you have to dig a little deeper to find."

I thought back to that conversation as I nodded a greeting to Jeremiah on that Saturday morning. I noticed one face in the crowd we were not familiar with, but we recognized the uniform. This Union soldier looked scared and confused, walking among the busy people of Gettysburg. His blue uniform was shabby, and he appeared exhausted and hungry.

Jennie walked up to him. "Hello, I'm Virginia Wade, and these are my brothers Samuel and Harry."

The soldier looked bewildered, but answered, "I'm Nat Tusker."

"Can we help you, Nat?" Jennie asked.

Nat looked at her with an expression of pure relief. "If it's not too much trouble, ma'am, I sure am awfully hungry. If you have anything to spare, I would be much obliged, and then I'll be on my way. I still have a long way to go."

"We have more than enough to spare," Jennie smiled. "Where are you headed?"

"I'm on my way to Virginia to join up with General Lew Wallace and the Eighth Corps."

Jennie caught her breath but maintained her composure. We hadn't heard from Jack in months. "I have a friend in the Eighth Corps," she said slowly. "If

I gave you a letter, could you at least try to give it to him? I would be so appreciative."

"I would be happy to, ma'am," Nat answered.

"Thank you very much." Jennie led the way home.

"Sure is beautiful countryside you have here," Nat said, when the silence became a little awkward.

"It's the best place on earth," Harry chimed in. "I bet heaven looks like Gettysburg." Jennie and Nat smiled at each other. It was sometimes hard to understand Harry, seeing as four of his teeth were missing.

When we had almost reached home, behind us we heard a lady's voice calling Jennie's name. We all turned and recognized Sarah Broadhead. She caught up with us, breathless.

She started to speak, but then noticed Nat Tucker standing with us. She curtsied and then went on talking. "Jennie, Jennie, have you heard the news? This very morning a message came from General Darius Couch, saying that we should see to our own protection. I knew it, I just knew it. Any day now there is going to be a battle on our own front lawns." Sarah put her hands in her face and began to weep.

I looked at Nat, and he appeared just as uncomfortable as me, shifting from one foot to the next. Jennie put her arm around Sarah and tried to console her.

"I'm just fearing for my children," Sarah choked out

between sobs. "They're little babies. There are just rumors of a battle, no one is quite sure, but I don't know what to do."

"Are you going to take General Couch's suggestion?" Jennie asked.

"There's going to be a meeting tomorrow night at the courthouse where the townsfolk are going to discuss it," Sarah answered. "I guess I'll make my decision after that. Will you be there?"

Jennie gave Sarah's hand a tight squeeze, "I will."

When we returned home, Mama was outside sweeping. She looked inquisitively when she noticed Nat. Jennie explained who he was and then went inside to fix him something to eat. Mama nodded and asked Nat if he would like to sit down.

John pulled up a stool and eagerly began talking to Nat about his home, his family, and being a soldier. I listened too, but I then heard raised voices inside. I went into the house to find Mama and Jennie discussing something they were both very passionate about. I stayed near the front door so I would not be noticed.

"We just can't make ends meet, Virginia," Mama was saying. "Ever since your father..."

I cringed. It had been thirteen years. I hadn't even been born yet when my father, James Wade, had stolen three hundred dollars from Samuel Durboraw. My father had claimed it had fallen out of Durboraw's pocket, but that didn't give him any right to take the money. He was arrested and sentenced to solitary confinement for two years. This devastated Mama, and through a complicated set of circumstances my father was declared insane and sent to the Adams County Alms House. I never really knew him, and because he couldn't support us financially, we suffered. Jennie had become a seamstress to help make ends meet, but obviously that wasn't enough. I even had to drop out of school early on to help support the family. Mama would visit him from time to time, but she always returned upset and never talked about it.

"I have decided," Mama said, "due to our situation, I think it would be best if we take in some boarders. What do you think, my dear?"

Jennie sighed. "I am inclined to agree with you, Mama." She poked her head around the kitchen door and saw me. "What do you think, Samuel?"

Ashamed that I had been caught without an invitation to their private conversation, I slowly walked into the kitchen. "I think taking on boarders might be fun."

Mama and Jennie exchanged smiles.

"Well, if our dear Samuel is for it and thinks it will be fun," Mama said, "I think I will make up an advertisement to put in the newspaper."

Jennie nodded and finished putting the basket of food together for Nat. I saw her take a letter out of her apron pocket and then hurry outside. I followed her.

Nat was still fascinating John with the tale of his life. Nat looked so much better than even an hour ago. His face seemed brighter and more full of life.

Harry, who had become bored with the discussion between Nat and John, had brushed off Nat's uniform and shined his shoes. Jennie smiled and handed the basket of food to Nat.

"Thank you, Miss Virginia," Nat said. "I will never forget the kindness of you and your family. Now, wasn't there a letter you wanted me to bring?"

Jennie gave him the letter. "His name is Johnston Hastings Skelly Jr."

"Is there any other message you would like me to give him?" Nat asked with a grin.

A little taken back, Jennie quickly answered, "No, it's all in the note."

Nat nodded, thanked us again, and then shook each one of our hands.

As he disappeared over the hill, Jennie put her arm around us. "I wonder if he will see Jack."

"What did you write in the letter, Jennie?" John asked in a teasing way.

Jennie's eyes twinkled, but she said sternly, "That is none of your business." She went back into the house.

Only Jennie, John, and I went to the meeting the next night. Mama stayed home with Harry. When we walked in, even though the meeting had not officially started, people were already speaking with raised voices. Jennie moved us along to find our seats.

A man called out, "Why don't we join up and protect the town of Gettysburg?"

"Yeah, send the Rebels back to where they came from," shouted another man.

Once again everyone began talking at once and I became, for the first time, a little frightened. I had never seen my neighbors and friends of peaceful Gettysburg behave like this. I guess when fear's involved, people do all sorts of things that go against their very nature.

"I say we all leave." I recognized Mrs. McCreary's shrill voice. "Get out while there's still time."

Others nodded and murmured in agreement.

"Wait, wait," John Rupp called out. "They're all rumors, just rumors! We still don't know if there really is going to be a battle in Gettysburg."

"But Governor Curtin suggested that we move our stores to a more secure place, and General Couch sent a message saying we should seek protection," Sarah Broadhead pointed out.

"That is just being overly protective," Mr. Rupp answered sharply. "Just in case there is a battle, they won't get blamed for not warning us!"

The room became abuzz once again.

With everyone talking at once, I did not know where to turn. I looked up at Jennie, and she seemed just as bewildered as me. John, on the other hand, loved a good debate and looked as if he was enjoying every minute of this rowdy meeting.

"Wait, wait, a cotton pickin' minute!" Someone yelled out amidst the chaos. I recognized the voice—Constable John Burns. He was an older man, almost seventy, with a fiery temper and a firm face. He had served in the War of 1812 and had volunteered in the Mexican-American War. Burns attempted to volunteer in this war, but was denied because of his age. Even though he could barely walk and suffered from ill health, the people of Gettysburg deeply respected him. Therefore, when he spoke everyone stopped.

"Where is everyone's spirit of patriotism?" he asked in his scratchy but still powerful voice. "Are you going to run away? Or are you going to stay here and defend our town?"

Everyone stirred uncomfortably in their seats. They remained silent.

"Are we going to get rid of these Rebels once and for all?" Mr. Burns challenged. "Or are *you* going to run away?" His emphasis of the word *you* sent a piercing dart to the hearts of the people, making the ones who wanted to leave Gettysburg extremely uncomfortable.

When we left the meeting that night nothing, even after John Burns's speech, seemed to be resolved. I was overwhelmed with a sense of fear and sadness.

Our town, which had always appeared to be close knit, was drifting apart. Some neighbors decided to take the governor's advice to flee the town and come back when things settled down. Others chose to stay in Gettysburg, either because they believed a battle was not going to take place or they did not want to be accused of being deserters. As we walked down the quiet, dark streets that night, neither Jennie nor John nor I spoke.

I felt a lump in my throat as I looked out into the dark fields and watched the slow fog creep up as if to embrace them. I wondered how soon it would be until those fields would be filled with soldiers and gunfire.

That night when I climbed into bed, I heard hushed voices downstairs talking very excitedly. When the voices died down I was still awake. John came up the stairs and tried to climb quietly in his bed, but I turned over.

"What was that all about, John?" I whispered.

Frightened by the unexpected sound of my voice, he spun around. "Nothing, nothing. Go back to sleep."

But after a considerable amount of prodding, John finally revealed to me that he had enlisted in Company B of the Twenty-First Pennsylvania Cavalry

Sorrow's Joy

I wondered how soon it would be until those fields would be filled with soldiers and gunfire

Regiment and had been assigned to be a bugler.

I stared at my brother in our candlelit room with unbelief. John, a solider? He was seventeen years old and barely five-foot-three. I had even passed him in height. He looked very much like Jennie, with a soft face, brown hair, and eyes that showed a compassionate spirit. He had a big heart and was loyal to America. Late into the evening, John quietly and slowly explained to me that Mama did not want him to go. She was afraid for him and had tearfully told him she did not want another one to go. John knew she meant Georgia's husband and Jack Skelly.

"What did Jennie say?" I asked.

"She was quiet for a while." John tilted his head, as if to remember the exact happenings during the meeting downstairs. "Then after a time she said, 'Mama, I think he should go. He has the same look about him that Jack had when he told me that he was going. It's a special look, the face of a patriot and a solider.'" John looked proud when he said this. "Mama finally said I could go, and she gave me her blessing."

"When do you go?"

"I'll be leaving on the twenty-sixth."

Five days. I had already said good-bye to two men who were like brothers to me. Now I was going to have to say good-bye to my real brother.

"Sure wish I didn't have to go so soon," John interrupted my thoughts. "If there is going to be a battle, I would want to be here."

I couldn't bring myself to answer. I turned back around and pretended I was going to sleep, but my dreams were plagued by battles.

A Mission for Me

I WOKE UP THE NEXT MORNING to the smell of breakfast. This aroma would on most occasions get me out of bed quickly. However, the events of last night made me want to stay in bed and sleep the pain away. But I dragged myself out of bed anyway.

Jennie was in the kitchen cooking. "Good morning, Sam."

I nodded and sat down.

Breakfast was extremely quiet that morning. Mama was at Georgia's house, so it was just Jennie, Harry, John, and I staring at our food. I noticed that Jennie did not say anything about John going off to war, so I assumed that John had told her I knew. Little Harry didn't know what was going on and why everyone was quiet and sad, but, being a very sensitive child, he never once broke the silence.

"We're going to have our first boarder," Jennie finally said. "Mrs. Brinkerhoff and her six-year-old son, Isaac. They'll be coming over later this afternoon. Mrs. Brinkerhoff works, so during the day we're going to have to look after Isaac."

How many changes had taken place over the last day? I wondered. *Maybe things will start getting back to normal soon.* I looked outside and spied John proudly practicing marching.

I sighed and murmured, "Maybe not."

"What's that, Sam?" Jennie asked.

"Nothing."

***

I soon learned that I had more good-byes to say. That afternoon, I took a walk and tried to sort through all these changes in my mind. I barely noticed a wagon pass me until it stopped. Out jumped Jeremiah.

"You going somewhere, Jeremiah?" I stared into the back of their wagon, which was packed full of their belongings.

"Yeah." He looked at the ground and kicked the dirt with his feet. "My family and I are leavin'."

"Leaving? Why? I thought this was your home."

"It is," Jeremiah replied. "It will always be, but with the rumors that the Confederates are comin' soon, my parents thought it'd be better to leave."

"Why?" I asked again. "They're coming here to fight, not to make you their slaves."

A Mission for Me

"Papa says we can't risk it," Jeremiah said quietly.

"Will you be back?"

Jeremiah shrugged and stuck his hands deep into his pockets. "I'm glad I got to see you 'fore we left. You been real nice to me, Samuel. I wanted to thank you for your friendship. Not many people got to know me, so I appreciate you takin' the time to."

I felt ashamed by Jeremiah's words. From my standpoint, I had not been a very good friend at all. The only time I had sat down to talk to him was that instant when we discussed his life back in Virginia. After that, all I would do was greet him when we passed on the street. He must have been so lonely these three years to think that I was a good friend. Now I wished I had taken the time to be the friend I should have been.

Jeremiah turned to join his family.

I stopped him. "Jeremiah?"

He turned.

"I could have been a better friend," I continued slowly not quite sure what words to say. "I'm sorry. I hate that you're leaving, but I have a feeling you're gonna be back and when you do come back, let's be real friends. I want to be your real friend." This little speech seemed insignificant and awkward to my ears, but as I looked up, I saw Jeremiah smiling.

"Write to me," I said, finding new confidence with his

encouraging grin.

"I'll do that," he answered. "And you write to me too and tell me what happens to Gettysburg."

"She'll be fine," I said. "We'll all be here when you come back."

"Jeremiah! Time to go," his father called from the wagon.

Jeremiah shook my hand and as soon as he jumped on the wagon, they were off, with Jeremiah waving from the back.

I waved too, until I could not see them anymore. Then I followed the ruts their wagon had left in the road for the rest of my walk.

What am I feeling? I unconsciously walked past the street where I was supposed to turn. I was not the type of person who did much soul searching, but I was confused at the deep, hollow feeling. Maybe it was unhappiness because so many good-byes had come and more were on the way.

No, it was more than that. The good-byes had fed into my feeling of despair.

Yes, despair was what I felt. Change. That was it. I was learning that I hated change. Even when the railroad came so many years ago, something did not sit right with me as I watched all the men and equipment roll into town. Also, when, little by little, the railroad began to be built, I did not like how it changed the

A Mission for Me

layout of our town. Sure, when I realized that excitement accompanied the new railroad, I did not dread it as much.

The change that had come with the war, however, was not followed by a thrilling feeling, at least for me. Because of it, I had to say good-bye to my brother-in-law and friend. I began to realize I was not as confident about Gettysburg's safety as I made myself out to be when I was saying my farewell to Jeremiah.

I was scared that this battle would change our town in ways I could not imagine.

***

Later that afternoon, Mrs. Brinkerhoff and her son came over. They looked uncertain standing in the doorway. Mama gave me a stern glance when I stared at them. Mrs. Brinkerhoff stayed in her room the whole rest of the day. I soon learned that Isaac was a sickly boy who was crippled. He had to be carried from one place to the next, but he and Harry enjoyed each other's company as they played outside.

The next day was Tuesday, and in three days John was leaving. I wanted to stay home from work because I wished to spend as much time with him as I could. But John was going to spend most of the day with his friends, probably bragging about his answer to the call of duty.

As I walked to work, I wished I could become more involved in the war effort. I wanted to do my part to put this country back together, North and South, but it seemed that throughout this war I would continue to be an errand boy.

The day went as usual except for the fact that each person I delivered to appeared nervous, and that was understandable. It's hard knowing that there is a possibility something is going to happen but not knowing when. At the end of the day I began to sweep the store, but Mr. Pierce stopped me and led me into his office. I was confused and wondered if this time I was finally going to be fired.

Mr. Pierce directed me to sit down. "You look at me, Samuel, and you just see a butcher."

I wasn't sure how he expected me to respond, so I first nodded my head then followed with a slow shaking of it.

"Well, I am not just a butcher," Mr. Pierce continued. "Have you ever heard of Zouaves?"

"Yes, sir. Zouave is a name of a regiment in the French Army that serves in French North Africa beginning in 1831, I believe."

"There is a Zouave regiment in Gettysburg too," Mr. Pierce said. "A volunteer regiment, one of many companies all over America—in New York, Ohio, Delaware, and even in California—all fighting for the cause of the Union."

I found this interesting, but I didn't understand what it had to do with Mr. Pierce being more than a butcher.

"I am part of the Gettysburg Zouaves," he said, "and I want you to join us."

"Me? A part of the war effort? In a real regiment?" I could hardly believe it.

"Now, now, Samuel," Mr. Pierce said, sensing my excitement. "You will not be fighting in any battles; you're far too young. You'll be more of a messenger for our regiment. We need more help, seeing as there might be a battle here soon."

An errand boy again, but for a much more worthy cause. I went home that night barely aware how late I was. Mr. Pierce and I had discussed the ins and outs of the Gettysburg Zouaves, what my specific role would be, and what was expected of me. I walked into my home, wondering if anyone was still awake or, more present on my mind, if any supper had been left for me.

As I stepped into the dark living room, I noticed a silhouette on the windowsill. By the light of the full moon I saw it was Jennie. She noticed me and motioned for me to sit down next to her. I did and explained why I was late.

Jennie sighed. I knew she must be thinking about all the changes that were happening to us because of the war. "I'm proud of you, Sam, but you must be careful." Her voice wavered. She quickly turned her face to look out the window.

"Jennie." I put my hand on her lap. "What's wrong?"

She turned to me with tears in her eyes. "I just hate what this war has done. It has torn people apart in one way or another. It has torn people apart in the form of North and South, it has torn people apart in the form of men marching away from their loved ones, and it has torn people apart in the form of those men dying, and they now will never be reunited with their loved ones on this earth."

I nodded, wanting to say words of comfort and hope to my sister, but none came. I just looked down.

"But..." Jennie continued wiping away her tears. "We have gotten through other tough times, so I am sure we can manage this one with the Lord's help."

"You still think of him often, Jennie, don't you?" I asked.

The name Jack Skelly didn't even need to be mentioned. Jennie leaned her head back. "Every minute of every day."

"What do you do when you miss someone more than words can say?"

"You hold on to the words they did say." Jennie smiled. Then she reached into her apron pocket and pulled out a letter. I recognized Jack's handwriting and gathered it was the last letter he had sent her.

Jennie then pulled a frame from her apron. The picture in it was Jack in his uniform. His face stared back at me.

"He's been gone so long I had almost forgotten what he looked like," I said.

"That's why I keep this picture." Jennie brushed some of my hair out of my eyes. "And you know something? I almost welcome this hardship of separation we have to endure, because it will just make our marriage stronger. I have learned that, sometimes, you cannot have joy without sorrow, or the joy is not as sweet."

We sat in the darkness awhile, until Jennie told me it was time for bed. As I walked up our creaking stairs, hoping I would not wake the boarders, I wondered what I would do without Jennie.

Friday, June 26, 1863

As long as I live, I will never forget that day. Neither would Jennie, I'm sure. The days leading up to it had been hectic. At first it had been hard living with the boarders, but we soon became used to it. Mrs. Brinkerhoff kept aloof and busy at work, but Isaac became a welcomed member of our family. He and Harry grew as friends and were inseparable. Jennie was in charge of the house because Mama was over with Georgia quite often. John himself became more and more excited as the day drew closer to his joining up.

I was learning the ways of the Gettysburg Zouaves, or the 114th Pennsylvania Infantry, which was their official title. I had met the others in the regiment and had gotten to know quite a few of them well in a short amount of time. They would tell me terrific stories of the battles they fought. Christopher was wounded during the Battle of Fredericksburg. David told me, in great detail, about the Battle of Chancellorsville, where their regiment suffered more casualties than they had ever experienced.

Friday, June 26, 1863

"It was horrible," he said as we sat under the shade of a tree. "Seeing your friends lying there on the ground. You can't stop and kneel beside them to see if they are really gone or to say your final good-byes. You just have to keep pressing forward. Our commander, Colonel Collis, collapsed during the battle."

"Was he shot?" I asked, wild-eyed.

"No, he had gotten ill a few days before and had insisted that he would continue the fight," David told me. "I was the first to see him fall. I thought he had been shot and when I could not find any blood on his person, I knew he was gravely sick. Thankfully, I was not too far from him and I was able to get to him quickly and take his pulse."

"You could feel it," I said, already knowing the answer.

"Yes, but it was faint." David explained how another soldier came to his side and in the thick of the battle they were able to get a stretcher and carry him off the field. "That was a mistake."

He didn't explain why carrying a deathly ill man away from a battle was such a grievous error, so I had to ask. "Why?"

David's face grew grim and he shook his head. "I have to say first that my head was in such a fog that I really did not know what was going on. All I knew was that Colonel Collis needed help. Before I knew it, five other men lifted the stretcher and he was taken away

Sorrow's Joy

David's face grew grim and he shook his head

Friday, June 26, 1863

amidst the smoke of the cannons and whizzing bullets. I learned later that the worst possible men took him off."

"Who were they?"

David pounded his fists together then ran his hand through his thick dark hair. "I hate it when good men are accused of doing bad things." He looked me squarely in the eyes. "Those men, who were officers, hated Colonel Collis. All of us knew it. As long as we could remember they had something against him and would do anything to ruin him."

"But they helped him during the battle," I pointed out.

"Yes, they helped him all right, but as soon as they could they falsely accused him of cowardice even though he had led and fought until he completely collapsed. He was brought to a court-martial and had to fight another battle, convincing everyone that he had done all that he could. He even asked me to be a witness, and I gladly accepted. I was proud to represent him, to clear his name and show them all that he had served faithfully. We won that fight, and he was able to return to his duty."

"Where is he now?"

"He was never able to shake off the illness," David responded wearily, as if he had put every last ounce of his being into clearing Colonel Collis' name. "He hasn't returned to us."

"Poor man." I reflected on David's story and all he and

Colonel Collis had gone through.

As though to change the subject, David said with a slight smile, "We're all glad you joined us, Sam. We're looking forward to getting to know you better."

"I am too."

However, one of the members I knew well. Far too well.

The day after I accepted Mr. Pierce's offer to be the errand boy for their regiment, he told me to come to meet the rest of the Zouaves. He said they would meet behind his barn. I was thrilled as I ran down the street. Finally I could do something to help the war effort. Yes, it was change, which I was scared of, but maybe this change would be good for me, the type that would grow me into a man.

I raced around the corner of the barn, and the first face I saw caused me to lose all my excitement. Franklin. He smiled when he saw me, but I did not return it. I searched the faces and found Mr. Pierce. I walked over to him and shook his hand.

He introduced me to the other men and they gave me a hearty welcome.

When it came time for Mr. Pierce to introduce me to Franklin, he chimed in, "Oh, I already know Samuel. We've been friends for years."

"Oh, well then"—Mr. Pierce clapped his hands—"I'm glad you already have a friend in this regiment.

Friday, June 26, 1863

Franklin, can you get Samuel's uniform?"

Franklin nodded and slipped into the barn. He returned with the most hideous thing I had ever seen. The trousers were blue and puffy, like breeches, with white leggings. The coat was also blue and fairly bearable, but it was adorned with blue cuffs and red trim. There were also yellow cloverleaf designs, which were made to give the appearance of large pockets. Worst of all was the hat. I was told later that its proper name was a fez, but it looked more like a turban to me, worn by those who lived in the Ottoman Empire, or so I had read. It was bright red and, worst of all, it had a yellow-gold tassel.

Franklin placed the uniform in my arms and stepped back. I rubbed my hands over it and then I ran my fingers through the tassel. I could not wear this. Then I looked up and saw the men smiling all around me.

"Is this some kind of joke?" I asked, barely able to get my words out.

Their smiles turned to frowns.

"This is the official uniform," Mr. Pierce answered gruffly in the same manner he spoke to me at the store.

"You should be proud to wear the same uniform as the 114th Pennsylvania Infantry," one man said. "Seeing as you are only an errand boy."

"It's historic," another said passionately. "The French units wore something similar in the colonization of

North Africa and the Crimean War. It's how we're known."

Wouldn't you want to be known by something not so colorful? But seeing that I had crushed these men's eager faces, and now knowing that this uniform was part of them and not a joke at my expense, I smiled.

"I am proud," I managed to say. "I am proud to wear this uniform and even...um...prouder to be part of this great and glorious infantry."

This was followed by a round of applause and I grinned, thankful that I had redeemed my first blunder.

"You're one of us now, Samuel." Franklin beamed as he stuck the fez on my head, and I didn't know if he was saying this in a teasing or welcoming way.

***

We all geared up for the battle we were quite certain would come.

But our town, oh Gettysburg, much to the dismay of Constable John Burns, was becoming void of inhabitants. People fearing for their lives had left. If someone had come to Gettysburg then, they would have seen a ghost town, with just a handful of people walking the streets with grim expressions on their faces, waiting for something to happen. The air felt heavy, like right before a storm with dark clouds forming in the distance. People kept their eyes on the horizon, wondering if the storm would pass over or

Friday, June 26, 1863

hit Gettysburg full force.

Jennie woke up earlier than usual that day because she had some sewing to do. John's uniform had arrived the day before. Unfortunately, it was two sizes too large. In his usual carefree way, John said it would be fine, but when he put it on and proudly stood there in front of us, we all had a hard time keeping back our laughter. John had never fully realized just how small he was. The blue uniform exemplified his small stature as he tried to reveal his hands, which were covered by the sleeves. The pants were no better. John had tied a rope around them to keep them up, and their length caused him to trip every time he walked.

Isaac finally said, "It's too big."

Jennie set out right away to alter the uniform. She had a few finishing touches to do on it the day he was supposed to leave.

I slept in that morning because I did not have to go into work until later that day. Right away I realized Mama was not there.

"She's over at Georgia's house with the doctor," Jennie explained. "The baby is going to be born today." I was excited, of course, but that day was hard because my brother was leaving.

John rushed in the door. "Are you almost done, Jennie?" He had just returned from Georgia's house to say goodbye to her and Mama. "I'm late as is."

"If I knew it was this uniform that was holding you back, I would never finish it." Jennie peered up at him and carefully snipped the last thread. "But I know nothing will keep you from going." Jennie held up the uniform.

John took it, thanked her, and went to go put it on. When he came back out, he looked like a soldier. Not just because he was in uniform, which made him appear taller, but because his whole demeanor was that of a soldier. Sure, he was scared. We had spent the remainder of his nights at home talking about the apprehension he felt mounting as the time for his departure grew nearer and nearer. However, John had reminded me of something Jack had told us before he left for war. Bravery was not the absence of fear. It was about being scared, but moving forward anyway.

I looked at John with my head cocked. "I wish my uniform looked like that!" Everyone smiled. A day didn't go by that I didn't complain about my uniform.

It was time for him to go. We stood outside to say our good-byes.

John constantly kept saying, "I'll be back. I'm gonna see you all again."

It took Jennie a while to release him from her hug, and when she did, he was off down the hot, dusty streets of Gettysburg. He turned to give one more triumphant wave and show us his unmistakable smile.

Friday, June 26, 1863

He turned to give one more triumphant wave

Later that afternoon, we received the news that Georgia had given birth to a boy and had named him Louis Kenneth. So our sadness mixed with happiness. We were just on our way over to meet our new nephew when we heard gunshots. We all dropped to the floor.

Sitting on the sofa, Isaac had panic in his eyes.

I stood, picked him up, and brought him down to the floor with us.

Against Jennie's wishes, I peeked out the window. A gasp came out of my mouth.

Hundreds of men filled the streets. Some were marching and some were on horseback. A number of them fired their guns into the air. It looked like a parade, but their uniforms were a most unwelcome sight.

They wore gray.

I relayed this to Jennie, who clasped her hands over her mouth.

Harry and Isaac asked a whole bunch of questions, to which Jennie could only answer, "It's started."

The streets were completely deserted when I went out a few hours later. Jennie begged me to stay inside, but Mr. Pierce needed me.

"Come, come in quick." He ushered me into his shop. "Samuel, I have a very important job for you."

Friday, June 26, 1863

He didn't even ask if I knew that the Confederates had come to town. Everyone knew.

"As soon as these Rebels came into town, they started taking all our best horses. It's terrible that they're going to use our animals for their nasty cause. Samuel, I want you to go back home and get your horse out of this town. Your horse is good and of some value, and I don't want these Rebels to make use of it. When you return, I want you to do the same with others in the village."

As I crept into our small barn, my heart was pounding. I didn't understand why, even though this was our barn, I felt like I was in a strange place. I moved slower to our horse with my shaky hand outstretched.

"Come on, boy." I tried to steady my voice so the horse would not sense my nervousness. But Blaze did appear nervous. He snorted and walked backwards.

"What's wrong?" I stepped closer. Then I heard a noise. Footsteps outside sounded closer and closer. I stood still, unable to move. The latch of the door was undone and I heard a creaking sound as it slowly opened. I held my breath then let it all out when I saw that was only Franklin.

"What are you doing, Franklin?" I hissed. "You scared me half to death!"

"Just seeing if you need any help," Franklin answered. "This is a big job. I'd be glad to help."

"Oh, yes, and then take all the glory!" I said bitterly.

"I don't know what goes on in your head, Sam." Franklin grunted. "You treat me so coldly and I just want to be your friend. I know when we were younger I treated you like a little boy because I wanted to feel superior, but that's all over now. Do you believe me?"

There was no time to contemplate if I believed or disbelieved Franklin. All I knew was that he did come over here to help.

"Thank you for your offer," I said with a hint of warmth in my voice. "But this needs to be my mission."

"Understood." Franklin smiled. "You've done well, Samuel." He turned and left the barn.

I carefully coaxed Blaze out of the barn and rode him down the still-deserted streets of Gettysburg to the Baltimore Pike.

I had almost reached the pike when I saw three men on horses approaching me from far away. The afternoon sun blinded me, so I couldn't make out if those men were friend or foe. At any event, they spotted me and came closer at a rapid pace. When they were right in front of me, I saw they wore gray.

"You, boy," the oldest solider said. His horse moved unsteadily from hoof to hoof. "Where are you going?"

I was so scared I felt paralyzed. I had never met a

Friday, June 26, 1863

Confederate soldier before. Finally, I found my voice. "I'm taking my horse out of Gettysburg."

The man scoffed and turned to the two others. "I don't think you are," he growled. "This fine animal and you are coming back with us. Ain't nobody allowed in or out of this town."

I had never been so scared in my life. Without knowing what else to do, I followed the soldier's order and handed him my reins and let them lead me to their camp. We did not go through the town, but as we made our way through the woods I caught a glimpse of it and wondered if I would ever see it again.

We reached the camp, and as we rode through, everywhere I looked I saw soldiers. Some were setting up tents, others made dinner over campfires, others leaned against trees telling each other stories, and many of them were cleaning their muskets. Some of them looked up with a questioning expression in their eyes when they spotted me. I could hardly believe I was in the Confederate Army's camp.

Eventually, the three soldiers stopped outside a tent. "Get down," one of them said, and I did. They pushed me inside a tent and then ordered the third soldier to guard the front of it. The two others laughed and led Blaze away.

I sat down in the empty tent, guessing this was the prison where I would be for I was not sure how long. How I wish I had let Franklin come with me.

I felt cold, even though it was over a hundred degrees out.

I felt scared, as I didn't know what was going to happen to me.

I felt sorry for myself, as I saw how alone I was.

I felt confused, wondering why the Confederate Army would want to keep me.

I felt ashamed that on the first mission I had been given, I failed.

I laid my head back and fell asleep.

I awoke to a familiar sound—Jennie's voice! I could hardly believe when I peered through a crack in the tent and saw Jennie pleading with the guard to let me free. I had told her I was going to bring Blaze to safety and had gone although she asked me not to. When I hadn't returned, she probably gathered information and learned that I was taken.

"Please, sir," she said, "he's just a boy. Please let me take him home. I promise he will not leave our home."

The guard continued to shake his head as Jennie implored.

Now I not only feared for myself, but for Jennie as well. I wanted to yell at her, telling her to go home and that I would be all right. But as I was about to, Jennie left. She turned to look back. I saw her wipe away tears, but she could not see me.

Friday, June 26, 1863

It was now late in the afternoon, and I suspected I had been forgotten. I sighed and observed that I could hear a faint sound of some men singing "Dixie."

"I hate that song," I muttered. I curled up and fell asleep again. This time I did not sleep for long. The flap of the tent was opened wide, letting in the afternoon sunlight. I squinted and saw the guard standing there. Still in a daze, I obeyed when he told me to get up.

We stepped outside. "On your way, boy."

I was confused. Why were they letting me go? "On my way?" I stammered.

"Yes, go, get out of here. We have no use for you."

I didn't wait for him to say it again. I ran off in a flash. Even though I knew these woods as well as my own home, because of my bewilderment and fright I could not remember where to go. Finally, I saw the edge of the forest and someone standing there. I ran into her arms.

"Samuel, Samuel, you gave us quite a fright." Jennie held me close.

"How did I get released?" I asked.

"Right after I left the camp, I ran to Mama, who promptly went to a Confederate General named Early and asked for your release. He agreed because he didn't even know why they had captured you, and here you are."

Even though it was childish, I let Jennie hold my hand and lead me home.

Because of my encounter with the Confederates, Mr. Pierce suggested that I stay with my family during the course of the battle. I think Mama had something to do with this sudden order by Mr. Pierce. I was disappointed to say the least, but I obeyed. I was going to miss all the action.

Three Days of Thunder

I AWOKE A FEW MORNINGS later and peered out my window to once again see soldiers marching down the street, but this time they wore a more welcome color. I realized, however, as I watched line after line of men pass, that there would certainly be a battle in Gettysburg.

On July 1, we sat at our table enjoying breakfast when a loud boom interrupted us. We all gave each other a frightened look. Everyone had terror in their eyes. The battle sounded as if it was just outside our door.

Jennie thought so too, as I heard her whisper to Mama, "We need to get to safety."

They decided Georgia's house would be safer. It was also decided that it would be less dangerous if we did not go all together. Therefore, Mama, Jennie, and Isaac were the first to make their way over to Georgia's.

As Jennie turned the latch to leave, I ran to her side, "I'm supposed to be the man of the house," I told her firmly. "I can take you over to Georgia's house one by one." I stood there looking into her eyes hoping my face did not reveal how frightened I felt.

Jennie did not talk for a long moment. She put her hand on my shoulder and whispered, "I need you to stay with Harry, Samuel, to keep him calm. I know you can do this. Will you?"

I nodded. Jennie turned and opened the door to the sounds of the battle.

As Jennie asked, I stayed behind with Harry to wait for her to return and retrieve us. Mama gave us each a tight hug and told us not to open the door.

Then they were gone.

Harry and I waited patiently on the kitchen floor for Jennie to come back. Harry had the idea that our brother John was out there fighting, and he continuously asked if he could go outside and find him.

"Just because there's a battle and John is a solider doesn't mean that he's in *this* battle. He's far away, Harry," I told him.

Soon Jennie ran in and closed the door behind her. The gunfire had been so constant I didn't even notice it anymore. But when she opened the door, it became louder, and I could hear men's cries and screams. I winced.

"There's a lull in the fighting, boys." Her voice had a hint of panic. "We need to go."

Three Days of Thunder

She quickly gathered some clothing and then locked the door behind her. We raced down Breckenridge Street and then made our way onto Baltimore Street. Gettysburg did not look like our town. It was hot and hazy, and smoke from cannons hung in the air. Porches on houses had crumbled. Many homes were abandoned and had holes in them from those cannons. Their doors were open and showed a disarray of items that had been valuables the day before but had been left when people ran, realizing that their lives were in danger. Worst of all, there were soldiers lying in many front yards. I could not tell if some of them were dead or alive. I could hardly comprehend what I was seeing, so I looked down and raced after Jennie.

We were all panting when we reached Georgia's house. Isaac's mother was there, cradling him in her arms. Georgia, still weak from giving birth a few days ago, was on the sofa, rocking a small cradle next to her.

Jennie went right to the kitchen to busy herself. Whenever she was nervous, she always did something in the kitchen to take her mind off her troubles.

The sounds of rifles and cannons continued throughout the day. No one in that house was able to set their mind on anything, except Jennie. She continually made bread for soldiers who kept coming to the door asking for food. These men looked completely exhausted as sweat dripped down them in their woolen uniforms. However, most of them appeared grateful as Jennie handed them the bread saying, "My prayers are with you."

Presently we heard more banging at the door. Jennie, wiping her floury hands on her apron, answered it. Not being able to see the person at the door, I got up quickly when I recognized the voice. Coming close, I noticed an old man dressed in dark trousers and a waistcoat with brass buttons. He had on a high black silk hat. In his hand was a flintlock musket like the ones used in the Mexican-American War. Old Mr. Burns.

"I couldn't help it," Mr. Burns told Jennie. "I was on my porch rocking chair when I saw it begin in the field across the way, and I thought, what a coward I was. How could I just sit there and watch all these men doing their duty while I rocked? So I grabbed my old gun and joined in the fight. General Chamberlain left the decision of my placement to Colonel Langhorne Wister, who sent me to the woods next to the McPherson Farm."

Jennie shook her head slowly in disbelief as she handed him some bread.

"Much obliged, ma'am," Mr. Burns smiled. "With this nourishment I'm sure to win this battle." And with that he was off.

"The Lord be with that crazy, brave man." Jennie quietly shut the door.

I later learned that the beginning of the battle was not

successful for the Union Army. The men had to retreat for their lives from Seminary Ridge and Oak Ridge to the south side of town.

"They are going to be thirsty in this heat," Jennie said. Before I knew it, she and I were out in the middle of the street offering water to soldiers running past us. Almost in a daze, I gave water to more men than I could count. Soon the soldiers did not seem like individual men anymore, but more like a steady stream of cattle running down the dusty streets.

Later, when I looked back on that afternoon, tears would come to my eyes as I thought about these men running for their lives as being sons, husbands, and fathers. It was strange to think about what they had just been through and, as I looked at them bedraggled, hot, dirty, stunned, and wounded, I had trouble considering that they were the "lucky ones," leaving their comrades on the field.

Being caught up in my work, I did not notice that Jennie had stepped away from my side. When I did become aware, I saw her on the side of the road bandaging a soldier's arm. She looked up at me and produced a slight smile. She looked so tired, dusty and dirty. She wiped sweat off her forehead as she tightened the cloth around his arm. I saw her lips moving, and I knew she was talking to him in her calm way.

We were certainly not done with our adventure, as we had to dodge and maneuver around the whiz of bullets to make it back inside Georgia's house. At one point we crouched behind a tree because there was intense fighting right before our eyes and right where we needed to go.

"Samuel," Jennie said in a hoarse voice as she tried to catch her breath. "If anything should happen to me, you just keep running. Don't look back. Do you hear?"

I just stared at Jennie, wide-eyed, unable to give an answer. She had spoken to me in her regular voice, but I could hardly hear her over the booming and crashing of cannons and rifle fire.

She grabbed my hand and led me away from our shelter.

Miraculously, Jennie and I did return home, but this was only to find Mama, Georgia, and Mrs. Brinkerhoff more anxious than before we left.

"The fighting is so terribly close," Mrs. Brinkerhoff wailed.

All of a sudden, a Confederate swung open the door. He glowered at us, and all we could do was stare back at him as if we were frozen.

He turned and, as if we were not even in the room, broke a window. The loud crash of breaking glass was no comparison to the noises we had been hearing for what seemed like eternity. The solider crouched and fired his rifle through the open window.

We all jumped.

"A sharpshooter." Georgia held little Louis close. "They've been going to houses without any warning to shoot the fleeing Union soldiers."

"I think it would be best," Jennie said without a hint of alarm, "if we made our way down to the basement. We'll be much safer there."

We spent the remainder of the day in the dark, musty basement with the noise of rifles right outside, sounding closer than ever before.

In the late evening, it all stopped. We still stayed in the basement until we were certain it was safe. Then we carefully and quietly made our way up to the first floor of the house. We soon realized the house had been in the middle of cross fire.

I nailed up a board covering the hole the Confederate sharpshooter had made in the window. I peered out the other window and saw bodies over the yard. I tried to eat that night, but the food caught in my throat. I looked around the table and saw it was the same for everyone else.

A sharp moan sounded. Jennie was the first to rise.

Mama put a firm hand on her arm. "No dear, please. Do not go out there again. Please stay inside."

"What if someone needs my help, Mama?" Jennie calmly answered. "How could I leave someone suffering right outside the door?"

Mama lowered her eyes and released Jennie's arm.

There was no stopping her daughter.

Jennie went over to the stove and took a biscuit and then grabbed a cup of water and some cloth.

I looked out the window as Jennie moved along in the moonlight around the dead to find the person who had made the cry. I saw her stop and kneel gently beside a solider. I craned my neck to hear what she was saying as she bandaged his leg.

"Here, have something to drink." She lifted his head for him to taste the refreshing water.

The solider did as best he could, but he soon started coughing and lay back down. "All gone," he moaned. "Everything is all gone."

Jennie put her hand on his forehead and smoothed back his hair. "Shhhh. You must rest."

"Where I'm going," the man answered, "I will have rest eternally, and I do think I'm already there because I see the face of an angel." He let out one final breath and was gone.

Jennie slowly dropped her hand from his head and sat there awhile. She looked up into the sky, and I knew she was praying. It was a sobering vision to see my sister so full of life and vigor sitting among the dead, men who had their lives snuffed out in an instant.

I later learned that the Confederates had just barely won that battle, but there had been unimaginable destruction and loss for both sides. July 1 had ended,

Three Days of Thunder

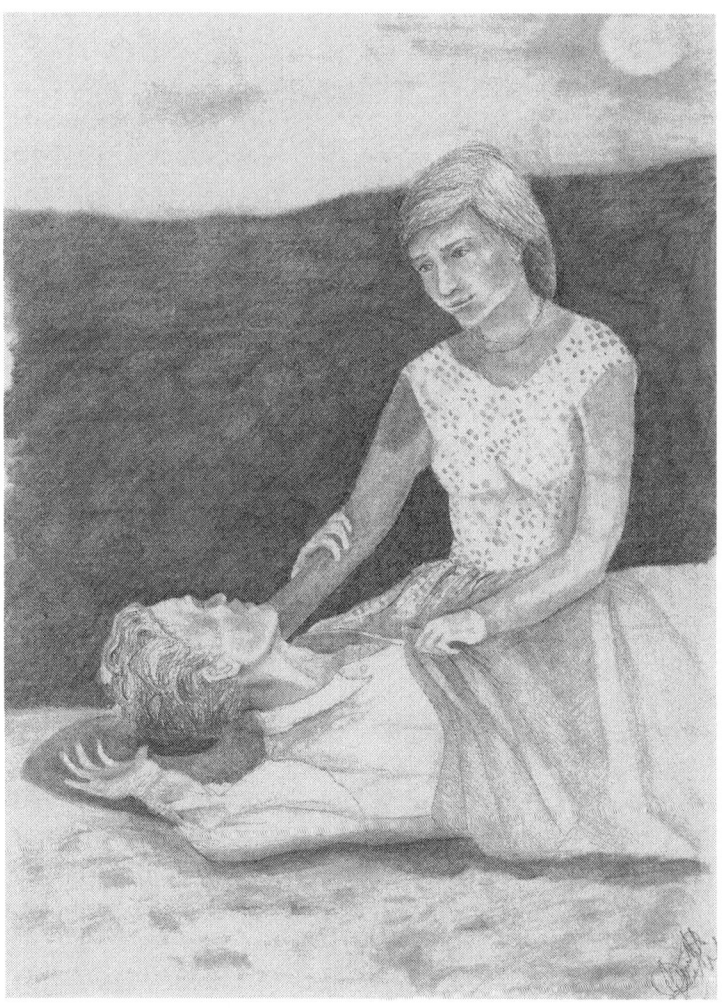

Jennie put her hand on his forehead and smoothed back his hair but the sounds of the next day were soon to come.

***

Thursday, in the midafternoon of July 2, we heard rifle shots close by. Afterward, I was told that General Lee's army attempted to attack the Union's fortification at Little Round Top, but they did not succeed.

Little Round Top held special memories for me and Jennie; it was our favorite place to go. Once you got to the peak of it, the view made you feel as if you were on top of the world and anything was possible. Jack Skelly would sometimes join us there, and we would sit on the rocks, eating apples and letting the sun warm our faces. The day before Jack went off to war, we all met up there again, and John joined us.

"You all are like family to me," Jack had said, with tears in his eyes. "And I can't wait until you are my real family." He smiled at Jennie, and she returned it.

John and I climbed down together that day. I looked behind me and saw Jack carefully helping Jennie maneuver around the rocks. She had such joy in her face as she took her fiancé's hand, even though she knew the sorrow that was coming.

During the battle, Henry and Isaac grew more and more frightened, so that July morning I tried to distract them from the piercing noise outside by talking about anything that came to my mind. The boys tried to keep up with my conversation, but their eyes would wander to the window when shots came closer.

I could not comfort them on my own. So I picked up the Bible from the table and began reading them the gospel of Matthew. After a time, Henry and Isaac settled in to listen to God's Word, which was the best source of comfort.

Mama, Georgia, and Mrs. Brinkerhoff listened, too. At one point as I read, I looked up at Jennie, who was kneading dough, and she nodded at me approvingly.

At that one point, peace seemed to be all around us, even though death and destruction were just outside the door.

The silence was soon broken by a loud, piercing crash.

We all fell on the floor as bricks, wood, and plaster rained down on us. Rifle balls had continually been hitting the house throughout the day, but this was a shrapnel shell hitting the roof. Miraculously, the missile did not explode. Nevertheless, the sound was so great the house shook. We all got up slowly and looked at the damage surrounding us.

Georgia shook her head in despair, her eyes wandering from the roof down to the floor. She let out a shriek when her eyes landed on Jennie, collapsed in the kitchen.

"Mama!" She screamed as she ran into the room and lifted Jennie's head into her lap.

"Oh, is the dear girl dead?" Mrs. Brinkerhoff wailed.

I pulled Henry and Isaac back as Mama ran into the kitchen.

Mama said, "No, she just fainted."

Jennie opened her eyes. We all let out a sigh of relief. Georgia fretfully guided her to a chair and put a wet cloth on her head.

"Really, I'm all right." Jennie looked at the five anxious faces surrounding her. "The noise just frightened me."

"All the same, dear," Mama retorted. "You are wearing yourself out. I will finish this last batch of bread, and then it is time for all of us to get some rest. I do hope the fighting is stopped for today."

An urgent rap sounded at our door. We all looked at one another, not knowing what to do. Another knock was followed quickly by three more. Without a word, Mama went to the door. We all held our breath and then rushed forward when we heard her shriek. There on the floor was a Confederate soldier.

"The poor man." Mrs. Brinkerhoff turned her face from the steady stream of blood dripping from his arm.

"He's fainted," I said, stating the obvious. "Or is he dead?"

"Help me roll him over, Mama," Jennie said. She saw Mama's worried look. "I feel fine."

They slowly rolled the solider over, and through the sweat, blood, and dirt on his face we all recognized Matthew McCreary.

"It can't be," Mama gasped.

"Who is it?" Mrs. Brinkerhoff couldn't have understood our sadness and bewilderment.

"An old family friend," Jennie said, half to herself.

Georgia quickly left the room and came back with a pillow that she handed to Jennie. Jennie put it under his head as Mama began tending to his wound.

I was still standing in puzzlement. Here was a Confederate soldier at my sister's door. What's more, he was our friend, who was now our enemy. Confusion as to how I should feel toward this helpless man crept into my mind. There was no question for Mama, Georgia, and Jennie as far as helping Matthew. Mama continued to clean his wound while Georgia and Jennie coaxed him to drink a little as he woke up.

"I tried to..." he said breathlessly, "I tried to go home, but...but...it was gone."

Georgia and Jennie's eyes met as they understood that Mrs. McCreary's house had crumbled to the ground in the midst of the battle. Thank goodness Mrs. McCreary had left town three days before.

That night, Matthew lay sleeping soundly in a bed. I crept past his room and peeked in, then slowly turned to leave.

"Sam."

I looked back.

Matthew was motioning for me.

Apprehensively, I walked close to his bed.

"It's been a long time, Sam," he whispered. "How have you been?"

Unable to answer his question because too many were infiltrating my mind, I blurted, "What's happening?"

Matthew produced a slight smile and leaned his head back on the pillow. "There's a lot happening," he replied, still in a whisper. "Do you mean what's happening as far as the past and why I joined the Confederacy? Do you mean what is going on as far as the war as a whole or just this battle?"

I shrugged. "I don't know. I'm just confused." I paused. "Tell me what you want me to hear."

Matthew, with a wince of pain, propped himself up. He turned to the window as a slight breeze blew the curtain in and out. It was the first cool breeze we had felt in a long while.

"I never thought I would come home like this," he mused, his head still turned toward the window. I waited. Matthew swallowed hard. "I don't have the strength to tell the long story why I chose to join the Confederacy, but I will tell you that was the hardest decision I have ever made. It was even harder..." His voice trailed off. After a while, when he turned back and faced me, he had tears in his eyes and he could barely speak the words. "It was even harder to walk the opposite way of my brother. I pray he's safe."

I stood there, uncomfortable. Matthew had always been a strong and unemotional man. It was strange seeing him so weak, helpless, in tears.

Changing the subject, I asked, "Can you tell me what is happening in Gettysburg right now? I can't even imagine."

"Death. Destruction. Chaos. What other words can I use to explain it?" His eyes filled with anger. "This morning I woke to silence. It was quiet. I had almost forgotten what nothing sounded like. There I was in the town where I grew up in the exact spot where I used to play as a boy. It was so strange to be in a place you had known all your life, but instead of a place where you and your friends pretend you are fighting a war, you all of a sudden find yourself not pretending anymore. We waited. What was to come next?" He sighed. "It happened this afternoon. The worst bloodshed I have ever seen. We were able to take control of Devil's Den, but what a cost! I was ordered, with others, to hide in the woods surrounding the field and to shoot any man who came as reinforcement. Through this I was able to get a good view of the battle. Smoke and screams, men falling and men advancing even though they knew that this could be their last step. It was all so..."

"It's all so horrible," I whispered. "How did you get shot?"

"I wasn't shot," Matthew shook his head. "It sure felt like it though, but it just grazed me. There was a piercing pain throughout my arm as I collapsed. I guess I passed out—probably from that pain and exhaustion. I don't remember much. Only that I could only think of home. Then I suddenly found myself here."

"You must have gone home," I remarked. "When you got here, you said it was gone."

"I must have then," Matthew whispered, sounding very tired.

It was time for me to leave. I turned to go. "Are you going to be charged with desertion?"

Matthew did not answer me. His eyes were closed.

Terrified that he was dead, I ran back over to his bed and slowly placed my hand on his heart. There was a beat, and his shoulders moved up and down in time to the breaths he was taking. I sighed and moved toward the door.

Mama was just coming in with a basin of water and a towel. She gave me a stern look as I slipped out of the room.

Later that night, Jennie still lay on the sofa while everyone else went up to bed. Mama was right, the fighting had stopped, but we were all certain that it was going to start again early in the morning. I sat by Jennie and watched her read her nightly devotion.

When she was done, she closed the Bible and looked at me. "Can you believe what we're going through?"

"You are certainly going to have a lot to tell your children," I answered.

Jennie smiled a little as she played with the tassel on a pillow. "Right now in the still and lovely silence of the night," she said quietly, "it's hard to believe that so much fighting, destruction, and death has happened during these past two days."

"I just can't wait until it's all over," I said. "This battle, and the whole war. Then everything goes back to the way it always has been."

"I don't think things will ever be the same again," Jennie replied. "Not after all this."

Yea, Though I Walk

The next day, Jennie took a break from making bread and sat everyone down to read to them as we ate breakfast. Georgia remarked that she was thankful she had stored up food in preparation of a battle so we would not go hungry.

Before Jennie read to us though, Mama informed us that Matthew must have left in the middle of the night.

"Did he go back to fight?" Isaac asked, with a worried look in his eyes.

"I do not know, dear." Mama placed her hand on his shoulder. "We will just have to pray that he is safe and well. We need to pray that for all the soldiers."

"Even for those who are enemies?" Harry scowled. "Matthew is against his brother and he would shoot and kill Louis, Jack, and John if he had the chance."

I looked over at Georgia and Jennie, knowing that these words heightened their fears for their husband, fiancé, and brother because I saw their eyes close and heads bow.

Mama quickly answered Harry, "Well, what does Scripture tell us? Love your enemies, bless them that curse you, do good to them that hate you, and pray for them which despitefully use you and persecute you."

Harry cocked his head as if he was thinking very hard. Then he turned to Jennie, "Do you pray for the Confederates, Jennie?"

Jennie stood up and moved toward the window. She did not answer for the longest time, and I knew she was still thinking about Jack. She turned to face everyone who had been silent, waiting for her answer.

"You know, Harry, I do have to stop myself from despising those who are my enemies. But then I think about those men and boys who are fighting on the same fields as Jack, John, and Louis, and I think of their loved ones waiting for them to come home just as we are. Then I pray. I pray that the Lord will keep all the soldiers safe and bring them home to those who have the same hope as me."

Harry did not answer, his eyes fixed on Jennie.

She smiled, "Did that answer your question?"

He nodded.

"I read this last night," Jennie continued, "and I thought you all should hear it. 'The Lord is my shepherd; I shall not want. He maketh me to lie down in green pastures: he leadeth me beside the still waters. He restoreth my soul: he leadeth me in the paths of righteousness for his name's sake. Yea, though I walk through the valley of the shadow of death, I will fear no evil: for thou art with me; thy rod and thy staff they comfort me. Thou preparest a table before me in the presence of mine enemies: thou anointest my head with oil; my cup runneth over. Surely goodness and mercy shall follow me all the days of my life: and I will dwell in the house of the LORD forever.'"

When she finished, we all sat quietly, listening to the noise we had become so accustomed to surrounding us.

"I wish you wouldn't read that," Georgia shivered. "It makes me terribly uneasy."

"How could it, Georgia?" Jennie asked with a furrowed brow. "These words show that no matter what happens, God will always be there because he is good. I don't fear death because I know that even in it, he will continue to care for me."

Mrs. Brinkerhoff trembled. "How could you mention death at this time?"

"Because I'm not afraid," Jennie answered. "If anyone in this house is to be killed today, I hope it is me, as Georgia has this little baby." Jennie took the baby from the hands of the bewildered Georgia and cradled him in her arms.

Yea, Though I Walk

"The Lord is my Shepherd"

"All the same, Jennie…" Georgia pulled the blanket closer around Louis's face. "I wish you would mind what you said."

We all sat in silence until a bullet ruptured through the window, causing a loud shattering of glass. To everyone's horror, it landed at the end of Georgia's bed where she was resting. We all thanked God that no one was hurt, and as Jennie swept up the glass I picked up the bullet. It was still warm. I decided to save it as a souvenir.

The day continued as the days before had, and I wondered how long we would be trapped inside.

"I'm going to bake some more bread," Jennie declared. "I'm sure we're going to have a lot of soldiers come today." With that, she walked into the kitchen.

Around eight o'clock in the morning I got up from the parlor to see if Jennie needed any help. Once again I heard a piercing sound, but this was different from the others, because it was followed by a loud thump. I ran into the kitchen with Mama close behind me. We stopped in the doorway, so shocked a gasp could not even escape from our lips.

On the floor lay Jennie, still with flour on her hands. Mama ran over to her and placed Jennie's head in her lap. With a bent head she felt for a pulse. Then, ever so slowly, Mama lifted her teary eyes and looked at me with an expression I will never forget. "She's gone."

I stood there, unable to move. No. My sister could not be dead. She was not part of the battle. She could not die. She was supposed to go home after this was all over. She was supposed to continuing sewing to help make ends meet. We were supposed to wait together for the return of John and Jack. She was supposed to marry Jack and have a family of her own. We were supposed to make a hundred more trips to Little Round Top together.

But all those "supposed tos" were gone, just like she was.

When Mama told Georgia, she let out a scream. In an instant two Union soldiers burst through the door. They took one look at Mama's face and knew what had happened. Their eyes landed on the figure on the floor.

"What are we going to do?" Georgia asked, her hand over her mouth. At that point, overcome by unspeakable grief, she left the room.

"Ma'am." One tall solider quietly turned to Mama. "We're going to have to do something with the body."

Still unable to grasp that her daughter was dead, Mama mouthed the words, "The body." Then, giving herself a shake, she answered. "We can put her down in the basement. But please, sir, take care and let me go with you; my daughter cannot be alone."

I spoke up. "I want to go with you."

Mama turned to me and nodded. Georgia came back

into the room, followed by Harry, who had not even seen our dead sister yet. His eyes were wide when he saw the two big soldiers in the kitchen. They then softened when he saw his older sister. All he could say was, "Poor Jennie."

"We'll come too, Mama," Georgia said.

Ever so carefully, Mama wrapped Jennie's body in a quilt. I watched as she, for the last time, held her daughter's hand, then released it. We all slowly descended to the basement.

The two soldiers cautiously carried the body down the dark stairway. They were followed by Mama, who wiped away tears, followed by Georgia, who held Louis close as she slowly put her foot on each step. I was behind her with Harry firmly clutching my hand. By the way he held my hand, it seemed as if he would never let go. At that point, I didn't want him to.

Jennie's body was placed in a wooden bench. Standing side by side, we all held hands as the soldiers closed the lid. For one last time I looked at my sister's peaceful face and knew that my life would never be the same, because part of it had left that morning.

Even though it seemed as if the battle was lost, the fighting continued throughout the day. Mama, using the dough Jennie had made early, baked fifteen loaves of bread. As she tearfully handed the bread to the hungry soldiers at our door I could hear her say, "My prayers are with you."

Yea, Though I Walk

The devastating Picket's Charge happened on that day, and the Battle of Gettysburg ended as a victory for the Union.

But from that moment on, I felt defeated. The Union might have won the battle, but for those in Gettysburg and, more specifically, the Wade family, we felt as if we had lost the war.

Finding Joy

ON THE FOURTH OF JULY, there were no fireworks, no speeches, no parade.

Everyone was just thankful the fighting had stopped. It had rained the day before, so the fourth was a hot, muddy, humid day.

The four of us stood together once again and watched Jennie's body laid to rest in Georgia's backyard. Four soldiers stood around us as two lowered the casket into the ground. We were all silent, unable to sing any songs or say any words of comfort.

However, the words, *Yea, though I walk through the valley of the shadow of death* kept reeling through my mind.

I never forgot my sister, who was beautiful both inside and out. I kept a picture of her in my pocket, like Jennie had kept a picture of Jack in her apron along with his letter. Jennie never wrote anything to me because we were always together. So instead of holding onto the words she said in pen and paper form, I kept all that she said in my heart forever.

Finding Joy

***

We all returned home, but it didn't feel like home anymore. The house seemed dark, quiet, and musty. Old familiar things that I had loved had lost their shine. Most of all, Jennie's smiling face was absent, never to be seen again.

We closed her bedroom and planned to never open it again. However, as more and more boarders came, we reluctantly concluded that it had to be used.

When I opened up the door that had been closed for many, many months to prepare the room for new boarders, I took a deep breath and realized it still smelled like Jennie. I would expect to see her each night when I came home from work.

I continued to be an errand boy for Mr. Pierce, both in his butcher shop. He forgave me for failing in my mission. He told me it was not my fault and that he was proud of my efforts.

Everyone in Gettysburg appeared as if shadows of death surrounded them. The town certainly had changed. Without question, it looked as if a major battle had taken place. Dead horses and bodies scattered the streets and the trampled fields. Many houses and buildings that had been standing strong and proud the day before the battle were damaged. The wounded were treated, and Georgia volunteered as a nurse. She continued to be a wise, comforting one for two years.

Sorrow's Joy

While the family tried to continue as normal, it was the most difficult and painful thing any of us had ever done. Sometimes I would glance over at Mama and find she had a faraway look in her eye, and I knew she was thinking about her daughter.

The neighbors tried their best to comfort us in our grief, even when they were living through their own nightmares. They would give a compassionate word or look as we walked to town or make a quick visit to our home to express their sympathy. Nevertheless, many did not know what words to say as it related to our unexpected tragedy, so they would not stay long.

I felt the most compassion and understanding from two very surprising sources: Franklin and Jeremiah. Yes, Jeremiah's family returned soon after the battle was over. His father was a great help in rebuilding our town, which was much appreciated by the townsfolk. I certainly appreciated what Jeremiah did for me. I was in such a daze after the battle, not really knowing where to turn or what to do. When the long afternoon would roll around, I would find myself sitting on our front stoop and watch the world pass me by as I was lost in my thoughts. At least three times a week Jeremiah would sit with me. At first, he would not say anything, but I sensed that he shared my sorrow as we sat side by side in silence.

One day as the sun was high above beating down on us he said quietly, "Tell me about her, Sam—only if you want to."

I sighed and told him that it was probably time to talk

about her. Where to start? She was a good sister, kind, understanding, strong and brave, which was demonstrated during the battle. I talked more than I wanted to, but once I started it was hard to stop. Jeremiah was a good listener, and these talks turned into longer conversations about other things. Soon a friendship that we should have had long ago began to appear.

Franklin had been wounded during the last day of fighting. Everyone was talking about how brave he had been, and I knew I should go and visit him. By the time I was walking up to his front door, I recognized that it was a much delayed call. His mother took me up to his room, where he sat on a chair. His face was very pale, and his arm was in a sling. He sat in a wheelchair, his pant leg folded up, making it clear that he had lost a leg. No one had told me the extent of his injury. Or I hadn't thought to ask.

He looked up as I entered and tears filled his eyes.

"I'm...I'm sorry this happened to you, Franklin," I stammered, trying to find the right words. The speech I had rehearsed on the way over sounded silly now that I was face to face with him.

Franklin shook his head and put out his hand. "No, Samuel," he said in a hoarse whisper, "I'm so sorry this happened to you."

Bewildered, I walked over and took his hand. His handshake was firm.

Sorrow's Joy

"Losing your sister," he continued. "It's not right. I'm a soldier. I'm the one who should be gone. Not a civilian, not a woman, and certainly not Jennie." He swallowed hard. "She was a good person, and although I can't pretend to understand your grief, I want you to know that I'm so very sorry."

I couldn't speak for the longest time. Here he was sitting in a wheelchair. He had lost his leg, and with it he had lost his dream of being a soldier. He had lost his independence. He had lost his ability to walk, forever a cripple. But through all this, his tears were for my loss.

Now I understood that I had completely misjudged Franklin. Far too long I had viewed him through the eyes of a seven year old looking up to an older, bossy, prideful boy who had transformed into a compassionate and caring young man. It was time for me to grow up and realize that not only do towns and lives change, but people do as well.

***

One day as I walked home from getting the mail, I kicked a stone down the dusty streets and thumbed through the letters. My hand halted over a letter that said, "From the White House." I ran the rest of the way home and placed the letter in Mama's lap.

Her hands shook as she lifted it up and read the return address.

"Open it, Mama." Harry eagerly leaned over her

Finding Joy

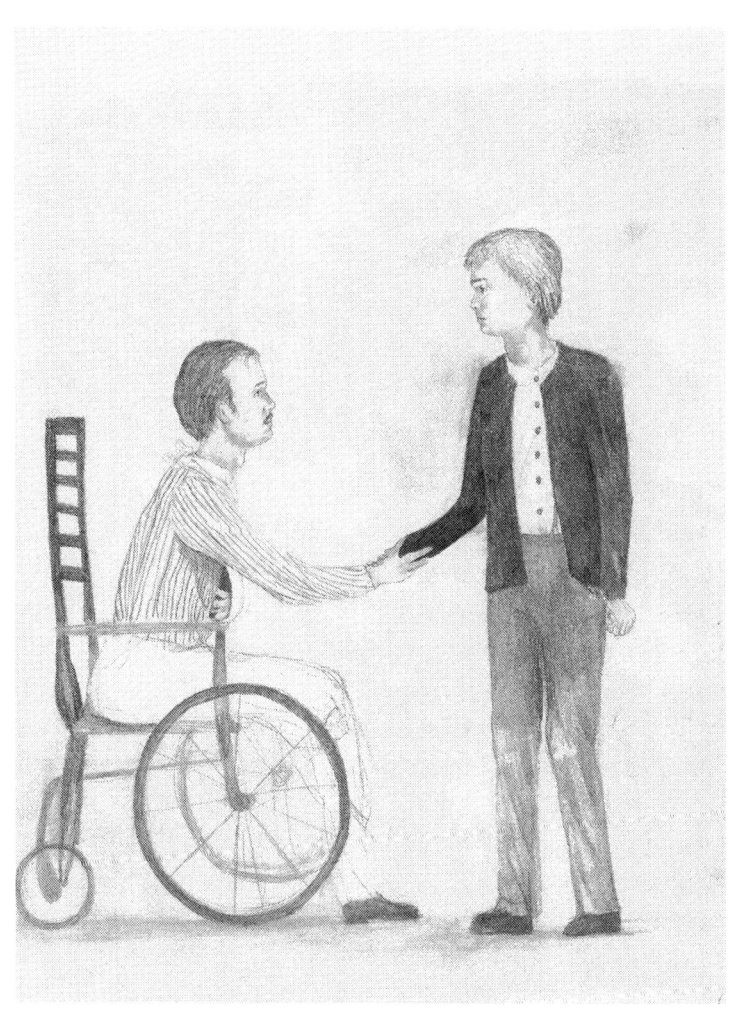

I couldn't speak for the longest time

shoulder.

President Lincoln's heartfelt and sorrowful letter praised Jennie for heroically dying while serving the Union troops. Mama read it to herself, then slowly and carefully read it out loud so Harry could hear it. When she finished, she took a handkerchief from her pocket and handed the letter to me.

"I don't want it to smudge." She wiped her eyes. I took the letter and ran my hands over the signature. *A. Lincoln.* I read the letter over and over again, desperately trying to pull some comfort out of his words, but none came. Even a letter from the President could not relieve my sorrow.

***

Summer drew to a close, but not the war. The hot air left, replaced by cooler gusts of wind. The leaves on the trees changed from green to auburn, yellow, bright orange, and when autumn itself was leaving us, for a time the wind picked them up and blew them away. Just as those leaves blew around the town, rumors also swept through the streets that the president would speak at the dedication of the Soldiers' National Cemetery. Sure enough, the rumors proved to be true. With that news, the saddened town began to be uplifted.

Because of her work as a nurse in the aftermath of the battle and because of Jennie, Georgia was invited to sit on the platform where President Lincoln was going to speak.

Even though she was excited, Georgia's grief was stronger. This was evident when she declared that day as we left together to go to the cemetery for the event, "It should be Jennie up there, because she was so much braver than me."

Practically everyone from Gettysburg was there, and Georgia slowly made her way through the crowd to the front. Mama, Harry, and I watched her with pride as she shook hands with the delegates and then the president himself.

A shiver engulfed me as I listened to the words of the president's eulogy, especially when he stated, "It is rather for us to be here dedicated to the great task remaining before us—that from these honored dead we take increased devotion to that cause for which they gave the last full measure of devotion."

Even though I knew he was talking about the brave soldiers, with his words I thought about my brave sister. Her devotion was as strong as any soldier's. She showed it all through those three long days as she kept her composure and wits even though she must have been as frightened as the rest of us. She showed it when she encouraged us with the steady Word of God as life around us seemed to be crumbling. She showed it as she stood in the dusty, hot streets offering refreshment to the soldiers in the way of water and her calm presence. She showed it as she continued to bake bread for the soldiers until the very last.

With these thoughts my mind had wandered, until

Mama took my hand and squeezed it. I shook myself and looked up to the platform, and my eyes met Georgia's. We seemed to be thinking the same thing. As eloquent and true as the president's words were, they did not help our grief. I had been trying to find words of comfort to take away the pain I felt, and I was looking in the wrong places. The words of sorrowful neighbors, my family, and even the president of the United States could not bring that consolation I desired.

I should have turned to what Jennie herself had read the day she died. "Yea, though I walk through the valley of the shadow of death, I will fear no evil: for thou art with me; thy rod and thy staff they comfort me." The Good Shepherd had acquainted himself with many sorrows while here on earth, and he was the only one who could provide the comfort I so desperately needed.

After the war ended in 1865, every day I saw soldiers come home to the arms of their joyful families. David and Matthew both came back home. Matthew never told us what happened after he slipped out of Georgia's home that one day during the battle. All we knew was that both boys were home and willing to start the slow and painful process of becoming friends again.

People would try not to be noticeable as they stopped and stared when David and Matthew would walk down the street together. One could see they were trying to mend their relationship. The joys they had as brothers before the war were certainly covered up by the sorrows of that war.

After some time, there was restoration in the McCreary household. One day, when I was on my way home, I passed by their house. David and Matthew sat on the front stoop, looking as if they were having an intense conversation. Matthew burst out in a boisterous laugh and slapped his hand on his brother's leg. David, the quieter solemn one, laughed as well, silently, but I could see his shoulders shake. At that moment, I witnessed old wounds healing.

I wondered though, when my wound would be restored.

Pain swept through me as I watched families reunite, because two people I knew were not coming home. One never marched off to battle, but the battle came to her and she felt the sting of war. Her fiancé never came home to see his Jennie. But they would reunite in another place.

I had kept the letter Jennie had from Jack in my top dresser drawer. I never read it. I was waiting to give it to Jack when he returned—until the sad day we learned that he would not be coming home. I was silent when Mama told me the news.

With no words to say, I quietly crept to my room. Without thinking, I walked over to my dresser and opened the drawer. There was the letter, still in its envelope. I took it gently and released the words that had been hidden away for so long.

Sorrow's Joy

Dear Jennie, *April, 1862*

I am hoping this letter reaches you. Words cannot express how much I miss you and long to be home. It pains me because I am not that far away from you, but this war makes the distance longer. Nevertheless, no matter how much I want to be home, I vow to be loyal to the just cause of the Union as I vow to be loyal in my love for you.

The days are long as our main assignment is just to guard the Baltimore and Ohio Railroad. You remember how much I hate to stand still. I wish I could see more action, although I know that worries you. But please do not worry for me; you just stay safe. How I wish I was there to keep you all safe, but I suppose, in a way, I am by being here. Through these sorrows we have to endure, I am certain the Lord is causing us to depend more and more on His might and through this, He is strengthening us. And I know our Good Shepherd is watching over you and we do not have to fear any evil because His rod and His staff will comfort us. Even if we walk in the valley, He is there. He is with us for eternity. As we will always be together; here on earth and in eternity.

Love Always,

Jack

I folded up the letter. The paper was wrinkled and worn. How many times had Jennie read these words? She must have believed what he said was true because she would say these things to me. I kept the letter and held onto it like a promise. A promise that Jennie and Jack were reunited and an assurance that I would see them again someday as well.

***

John did come home.

I waited for him as he walked up the path to our house. When he became close, I noticed he lingered, and I knew he was thinking about her.

A few days later, we went to visit her grave. It had been moved to the cemetery where Abraham Lincoln had spoken and where all the other brave soldiers were laid to rest. We knelt silently, and John placed a single rose in front of it.

"She was a good sister." I peered at John's bent head. "Was. I hate that word, because it means something is over."

"True," John said, after a time. "But that word doesn't always mean something bad if something good follows. I was gone, but now I'm home. The war was more horrible than words can say, but the North won and the Union is saved. I do know what you mean, but I'd rather have had Jennie for the short time we did than not have her at all. Even if I have to say, 'She was a good sister.'"

"You can't have joy without sorrow," I mused.

It took me years to fully understand what he said. It took me years of hurt, anger, and sadness to find the joy heavily buried beneath the sorrow of Jennie's death. I finally did grasp the joy that could be found in her death. Just as John said about himself, Jennie was gone, but, in the same sense, she was also home.

That was the joy amidst the sorrow.

A TRUTHFUL TALE

*Gettysburg, home of many abolitionists, was really part of the Underground Railroad.

*Johnston Hasting "Jack" Skelly Jr. was a longtime friend of the Wade family. Friends since childhood, he and Jennie fell in love and indications show that they were to marry. Skelly served his country in the Eighth Corps in Virginia, giving his life for the cause of the Union around the time of his beloved Jennie's death.

*Samuel Wade worked for James Pierce's butcher shop and volunteered for the Gettysburg Zouaves. He was captured by Confederates while smuggling horses out of Gettysburg. The Confederates came, his nephew was born and his brother went off to war all in the same day.

*At the age of sixty-nine, Constable John Burns watched the battle from his front porch rocking chair. Wanting to become part of the action, he grabbed his musket and joined the fight.

*Jennie tirelessly baked bread for the famished soldiers as they came running to her door during the Battle of Gettysburg. She would also tend to soldiers who were wounded on the front lawn. Throughout the battle, she diligently stood out in the street handing water to the steady stream of men running past her during one of the worst days of their lives.

*Jennie's Bible was opened to the 23rd Psalm when the fateful bullet tore through the house.

*President Abraham Lincoln wrote a letter to the Wade family thanking them for Jennie's service and expressing his sorrow for their loss.

*Georgia McClellan became a nurse following the death of her sister. President Lincoln invited her to be present when he gave his now famous Gettysburg Address.

The Battle of Gettysburg Highlights

July 1st- The first clash begins in the morning near McPherson's Ridge. Later in the afternoon, the Confederates troops force the Unions to retreat to Cemetery Hill.

July 2nd- Going against orders, General Daniel Sickles calls the troops to leave Cemetery Ridge and head toward the Peach Orchard. This is unsuccessful and, that night, they retreat back to Cemetery Ridge. On the Confederates side, troops attack on Little Round Top and try to take it over, but this is unsuccessful. Moreover, there is a brawl at Delvin's Den resulting with the Confederates being the victor.

July 3rd- Fighting begins early in the morning at the bottom of Culp's Hill and the Confederates are driven back. The costly and overwhelming defeat of Pickett's Charge takes place in the early afternoon. Charging across open fields, Confederates troops are vulnerable targets and in an hour, half of them are wounded or dead. Later that afternoon, Confederates begin to make their final retreat. That morning, Jennie Wade is hit and killed by a sniper's bullet.

Made in the USA
Lexington, KY
27 April 2016